About My Blog

Purpose Of My Blog	Why does your blog exist?
Target Audience	Who do want to attract?
What I Offer	What do you offer your readers?
How I Promote	How do you promote your blog?
Money	Do you monetize your blog? How?

My Blog Categories

Category #1

Sub-Categories
- ○
- ○
- ○

Category #2

Sub-Categories
- ○
- ○
- ○

Category #3

Sub-Categories
- ○
- ○
- ○

Category #4

Sub-Categories
- ○
- ○
- ○

Category #5

Sub-Categories
- ○
- ○
- ○

Category #6

Sub-Categories
- ○
- ○
- ○

Blog Tags I Use

Tag	In Category	For Topic

Blog Post Index

✓	Post Title	Category	Pages

✓	Post Title	Category	Pages

	Blog title:	

Publish date:	Category:

Quick Post Summary	What exactly are you aiming for?

Main Keywords	SEO	Pinterest
	○	○
	○	○
	○	○
	○	○
	○	○

Opt-in Offer	Are you offering a freebie/upgrade?

Heading #1	
Heading #2	
Heading #3	
Heading #4	
Heading #5	

Research Points

What research is needed for this?

-
-
-
-

Affiliate Products

Are you promoting any products?

-
-
-
-

Social Media Plan

What's the social media plan for this?

Blog Post Checklist

○ Catchy title	○ Descriptions written
○ Keyworded	○ Affiliate links added
○ Images made	○ Internal links
○ Headings	○ Call to action
○ Checked & edited	○ Social media scheduled
○	○
○	○

Blog title:

Publish date: | **Category:**

Quick Post Summary

What exactly are you aiming for?

Main Keywords

SEO	Pinterest
○	○
○	○
○	○
○	○
○	○

Opt-in Offer

Are you offering a freebie/upgrade?

Heading #1

Heading #2

Heading #3

Heading #4

Heading #5

Research Points

What research is needed for this?

- ○
- ○
- ○
- ○

Affiliate Products

Are you promoting any products?

- ○
- ○
- ○
- ○

Social Media Plan

What's the social media plan for this?

Blog Post Checklist	
○ Catchy title	○ Descriptions written
○ Keyworded	○ Affiliate links added
○ Images made	○ Internal links
○ Headings	○ Call to action
○ Checked & edited	○ Social media scheduled
○	○
○	○

Blog title:

Publish date: **Category:**

Quick Post Summary

What exactly are you aiming for?

Main Keywords

SEO	Pinterest
○	○
○	○
○	○
○	○
○	○

Opt-in Offer

Are you offering a freebie/upgrade?

Heading #1

Heading #2

Heading #3

Heading #4

Heading #5

Research Points

What research is needed for this?

- ○
- ○
- ○
- ○

Affiliate Products

Are you promoting any products?

- ○
- ○
- ○
- ○

Social Media Plan

What's the social media plan for this?

Blog Post Checklist

○ Catchy title	○ Descriptions written
○ Keyworded	○ Affiliate links added
○ Images made	○ Internal links
○ Headings	○ Call to action
○ Checked & edited	○ Social media scheduled
○	○
○	○

◯ Blog title:	

Publish date:	Category:

Quick Post Summary	What exactly are you aiming for?

Main Keywords	SEO	Pinterest
	◦	◦
	◦	◦
	◦	◦
	◦	◦
	◦	◦

Opt-in Offer	Are you offering a freebie/upgrade?

Heading #1	
Heading #2	
Heading #3	
Heading #4	
Heading #5	

Research Points

What research is needed for this?

- ○
- ○
- ○
- ○

Affiliate Products

Are you promoting any products?

- ○
- ○
- ○
- ○

Social Media Plan

What's the social media plan for this?

Blog Post Checklist

○	Catchy title	○	Descriptions written
○	Keyworded	○	Affiliate links added
○	Images made	○	Internal links
○	Headings	○	Call to action
○	Checked & edited	○	Social media scheduled
○		○	
○		○	

Blog title:

Publish date: | **Category:**

Quick Post Summary | What exactly are you aiming for?

Main Keywords

SEO	Pinterest
○	○
○	○
○	○
○	○
○	○

Opt-in Offer | Are you offering a freebie/upgrade?

Heading #1

Heading #2

Heading #3

Heading #4

Heading #5

Research Points

What research is needed for this?

-
-
-
-

Affiliate Products

Are you promoting any products?

-
-
-
-

Social Media Plan

What's the social media plan for this?

Blog Post Checklist	
○ Catchy title	○ Descriptions written
○ Keyworded	○ Affiliate links added
○ Images made	○ Internal links
○ Headings	○ Call to action
○ Checked & edited	○ Social media scheduled
○	○
○	○

Blog title:	

Publish date:	**Category:**

Quick Post Summary	What exactly are you aiming for?

	SEO	Pinterest
Main Keywords	○ ○ ○ ○ ○	○ ○ ○ ○ ○

Opt-in Offer	Are you offering a freebie/upgrade?

Heading #1	
Heading #2	
Heading #3	
Heading #4	
Heading #5	

Research Points

What research is needed for this?

- ○
- ○
- ○
- ○

Affiliate Products

Are you promoting any products?

- ○
- ○
- ○
- ○

Social Media Plan

What's the social media plan for this?

Blog Post Checklist

○	Catchy title	○	Descriptions written
○	Keyworded	○	Affiliate links added
○	Images made	○	Internal links
○	Headings	○	Call to action
○	Checked & edited	○	Social media scheduled
○		○	
○		○	

Blog title:	

Publish date: | **Category:** |

Quick Post Summary	What exactly are you aiming for?

	SEO	Pinterest
Main Keywords	○ ○ ○ ○ ○	○ ○ ○ ○ ○

Opt-in Offer	Are you offering a freebie/upgrade?

Heading #1	
Heading #2	
Heading #3	
Heading #4	
Heading #5	

Research Points

What research is needed for this?

- ○
- ○
- ○
- ○

Affiliate Products

Are you promoting any products?

- ○
- ○
- ○
- ○

Social Media Plan

What's the social media plan for this?

Blog Post Checklist

○ Catchy title	○ Descriptions written
○ Keyworded	○ Affiliate links added
○ Images made	○ Internal links
○ Headings	○ Call to action
○ Checked & edited	○ Social media scheduled
○	○
○	○

○ Blog title:	

Publish date:	Category:	

Quick Post Summary	What exactly are you aiming for?

Main Keywords	SEO	Pinterest
	○	○
	○	○
	○	○
	○	○
	○	○

Opt-in Offer	Are you offering a freebie/upgrade?

Heading #1	
Heading #2	
Heading #3	
Heading #4	
Heading #5	

Research Points

What research is needed for this? ◯

- ○
- ○
- ○
- ○

Affiliate Products

Are you promoting any products?

- ○
- ○
- ○
- ○

Social Media Plan

What's the social media plan for this?

Blog Post Checklist

○	Catchy title	○	Descriptions written
○	Keyworded	○	Affiliate links added
○	Images made	○	Internal links
○	Headings	○	Call to action
○	Checked & edited	○	Social media scheduled
○		○	
○		○	

Blog title:

Publish date: | **Category:**

Quick Post Summary

What exactly are you aiming for?

Main Keywords

SEO	Pinterest
○	○
○	○
○	○
○	○
○	○

Opt-in Offer

Are you offering a freebie/upgrade?

Heading #1

Heading #2

Heading #3

Heading #4

Heading #5

Research Points

What research is needed for this?

○
○
○
○

Affiliate Products

Are you promoting any products?

○
○
○
○

Social Media Plan

What's the social media plan for this?

Blog Post Checklist	
○ Catchy title	○ Descriptions written
○ Keyworded	○ Affiliate links added
○ Images made	○ Internal links
○ Headings	○ Call to action
○ Checked & edited	○ Social media scheduled
○	○
○	○

◯ Blog title:	

Publish date:	Category:

Quick Post Summary	What exactly are you aiming for?

	SEO	Pinterest
Main Keywords	◯ ◯ ◯ ◯ ◯	◯ ◯ ◯ ◯ ◯

Opt-in Offer	Are you offering a freebie/upgrade?

Heading #1	
Heading #2	
Heading #3	
Heading #4	
Heading #5	

Research Points

What research is needed for this?

- ○
- ○
- ○
- ○

Affiliate Products

Are you promoting any products?

- ○
- ○
- ○
- ○

Social Media Plan

What's the social media plan for this?

Blog Post Checklist	
○ Catchy title	○ Descriptions written
○ Keyworded	○ Affiliate links added
○ Images made	○ Internal links
○ Headings	○ Call to action
○ Checked & edited	○ Social media scheduled
○	○
○	○

Blog title:

Publish date: **Category:**

Quick Post Summary | What exactly are you aiming for?

Main Keywords

	SEO		Pinterest
	○		○
	○		○
	○		○
	○		○
	○		○

Opt-in Offer | Are you offering a freebie/upgrade?

Heading #1

Heading #2

Heading #3

Heading #4

Heading #5

Research Points

What research is needed for this?

- ○
- ○
- ○
- ○

Affiliate Products

Are you promoting any products?

- ○
- ○
- ○
- ○

Social Media Plan

What's the social media plan for this?

Blog Post Checklist	
○ Catchy title	○ Descriptions written
○ Keyworded	○ Affiliate links added
○ Images made	○ Internal links
○ Headings	○ Call to action
○ Checked & edited	○ Social media scheduled
○	○
○	○

Blog title:

Publish date: | **Category:**

Quick Post Summary

What exactly are you aiming for?

Main Keywords

SEO	Pinterest
○	○
○	○
○	○
○	○
○	○

Opt-in Offer

Are you offering a freebie/upgrade?

Heading #1

Heading #2

Heading #3

Heading #4

Heading #5

Research Points

What research is needed for this?

- ○
- ○
- ○
- ○

Affiliate Products

Are you promoting any products?

- ○
- ○
- ○
- ○

Social Media Plan

What's the social media plan for this?

Blog Post Checklist

○ Catchy title	○ Descriptions written
○ Keyworded	○ Affiliate links added
○ Images made	○ Internal links
○ Headings	○ Call to action
○ Checked & edited	○ Social media scheduled
○	○
○	○

Blog title:

Publish date: | **Category:**

Quick Post Summary | What exactly are you aiming for?

Main Keywords

	SEO		Pinterest
	○		○
	○		○
	○		○
	○		○
	○		○

Opt-in Offer | Are you offering a freebie/upgrade?

Heading #1

Heading #2

Heading #3

Heading #4

Heading #5

Research Points

What research is needed for this? ◯

- ○
- ○
- ○
- ○

Affiliate Products

Are you promoting any products?

- ○
- ○
- ○
- ○

Social Media Plan

What's the social media plan for this?

Blog Post Checklist	
○ Catchy title	○ Descriptions written
○ Keyworded	○ Affiliate links added
○ Images made	○ Internal links
○ Headings	○ Call to action
○ Checked & edited	○ Social media scheduled
○	○
○	○

Blog title:

Publish date: | **Category:**

Quick Post Summary — What exactly are you aiming for?

Main Keywords

SEO	Pinterest
○	○
○	○
○	○
○	○
○	○

Opt-in Offer — Are you offering a freebie/upgrade?

Heading #1

Heading #2

Heading #3

Heading #4

Heading #5

Research Points

What research is needed for this?

- ◯
- ◯
- ◯
- ◯

Affiliate Products

Are you promoting any products?

- ◯
- ◯
- ◯
- ◯

Social Media Plan

What's the social media plan for this?

Blog Post Checklist	
◯ Catchy title	◯ Descriptions written
◯ Keyworded	◯ Affiliate links added
◯ Images made	◯ Internal links
◯ Headings	◯ Call to action
◯ Checked & edited	◯ Social media scheduled
◯	◯
◯	◯

Blog title:

Publish date: **Category:**

Quick Post Summary

What exactly are you aiming for?

Main Keywords

SEO	Pinterest
○	○
○	○
○	○
○	○
○	○

Opt-in Offer

Are you offering a freebie/upgrade?

Heading #1

Heading #2

Heading #3

Heading #4

Heading #5

Research Points

What research is needed for this?

- ○
- ○
- ○
- ○

Affiliate Products

Are you promoting any products?

- ○
- ○
- ○
- ○

Social Media Plan

What's the social media plan for this?

Blog Post Checklist	
○ Catchy title	○ Descriptions written
○ Keyworded	○ Affiliate links added
○ Images made	○ Internal links
○ Headings	○ Call to action
○ Checked & edited	○ Social media scheduled
○	○
○	○

Blog title:

Publish date: | **Category:**

Quick Post Summary

What exactly are you aiming for?

Main Keywords

SEO	Pinterest
○	○
○	○
○	○
○	○
○	○

Opt-in Offer

Are you offering a freebie/upgrade?

Heading #1

Heading #2

Heading #3

Heading #4

Heading #5

Research Points

What research is needed for this?

- ○
- ○
- ○
- ○

Affiliate Products

Are you promoting any products?

- ○
- ○
- ○
- ○

Social Media Plan

What's the social media plan for this?

Blog Post Checklist	
○ Catchy title	○ Descriptions written
○ Keyworded	○ Affiliate links added
○ Images made	○ Internal links
○ Headings	○ Call to action
○ Checked & edited	○ Social media scheduled
○	○
○	○

Blog title:

Publish date: **Category:**

Quick Post Summary

What exactly are you aiming for?

Main Keywords

SEO	Pinterest
○	○
○	○
○	○
○	○
○	○

Opt-in Offer

Are you offering a freebie/upgrade?

Heading #1

Heading #2

Heading #3

Heading #4

Heading #5

Research Points

What research is needed for this?

- ○
- ○
- ○
- ○

Affiliate Products

Are you promoting any products?

- ○
- ○
- ○
- ○

Social Media Plan

What's the social media plan for this?

Blog Post Checklist	
○ Catchy title	○ Descriptions written
○ Keyworded	○ Affiliate links added
○ Images made	○ Internal links
○ Headings	○ Call to action
○ Checked & edited	○ Social media scheduled
○	○
○	○

Blog title:

Publish date: | **Category:**

Quick Post Summary

What exactly are you aiming for?

Main Keywords

SEO	Pinterest
○	○
○	○
○	○
○	○
○	○

Opt-in Offer

Are you offering a freebie/upgrade?

Heading #1

Heading #2

Heading #3

Heading #4

Heading #5

Research Points

What research is needed for this?

- ○
- ○
- ○
- ○

Affiliate Products

Are you promoting any products?

- ○
- ○
- ○
- ○

Social Media Plan

What's the social media plan for this?

Blog Post Checklist	
○ Catchy title	○ Descriptions written
○ Keyworded	○ Affiliate links added
○ Images made	○ Internal links
○ Headings	○ Call to action
○ Checked & edited	○ Social media scheduled
○	○
○	○

	Blog title:	

Publish date:	**Category:**

Quick Post Summary	What exactly are you aiming for?

Main Keywords	SEO	Pinterest
	○	○
	○	○
	○	○
	○	○
	○	○

Opt-in Offer	Are you offering a freebie/upgrade?

Heading #1	
Heading #2	
Heading #3	
Heading #4	
Heading #5	

Research Points

What research is needed for this?

- ○
- ○
- ○
- ○

Affiliate Products

Are you promoting any products?

- ○
- ○
- ○
- ○

Social Media Plan

What's the social media plan for this?

Blog Post Checklist

○ Catchy title	○ Descriptions written
○ Keyworded	○ Affiliate links added
○ Images made	○ Internal links
○ Headings	○ Call to action
○ Checked & edited	○ Social media scheduled
○	○
○	○

⬤ Blog title:	

Publish date:	Category:

Quick Post Summary	What exactly are you aiming for?

Main Keywords	SEO	Pinterest
	○	○
	○	○
	○	○
	○	○
	○	○

Opt-in Offer	Are you offering a freebie/upgrade?

Heading #1	
Heading #2	
Heading #3	
Heading #4	
Heading #5	

Research Points

What research is needed for this? ◯

- ○
- ○
- ○
- ○

Affiliate Products

Are you promoting any products?

- ○
- ○
- ○
- ○

Social Media Plan

What's the social media plan for this?

Blog Post Checklist

○	Catchy title	○	Descriptions written
○	Keyworded	○	Affiliate links added
○	Images made	○	Internal links
○	Headings	○	Call to action
○	Checked & edited	○	Social media scheduled
○		○	
○		○	

◯ Blog title:	

Publish date:	Category:

Quick Post Summary	What exactly are you aiming for?

	SEO	Pinterest
Main Keywords	◯ ◯ ◯ ◯ ◯	◯ ◯ ◯ ◯ ◯

Opt-in Offer	Are you offering a freebie/upgrade?

Heading #1	
Heading #2	
Heading #3	
Heading #4	
Heading #5	

Research Points

What research is needed for this?

- ○
- ○
- ○
- ○

Affiliate Products

Are you promoting any products?

- ○
- ○
- ○
- ○

Social Media Plan

What's the social media plan for this?

Blog Post Checklist

○ Catchy title	○ Descriptions written
○ Keyworded	○ Affiliate links added
○ Images made	○ Internal links
○ Headings	○ Call to action
○ Checked & edited	○ Social media scheduled
○	○
○	○

Blog title:

Publish date: | **Category:**

Quick Post Summary

What exactly are you aiming for?

Main Keywords

SEO	Pinterest
○	○
○	○
○	○
○	○
○	○

Opt-in Offer

Are you offering a freebie/upgrade?

Heading #1

Heading #2

Heading #3

Heading #4

Heading #5

Research Points

What research is needed for this?

- ○
- ○
- ○
- ○

Affiliate Products

Are you promoting any products?

- ○
- ○
- ○
- ○

Social Media Plan

What's the social media plan for this?

Blog Post Checklist

○	Catchy title	○	Descriptions written
○	Keyworded	○	Affiliate links added
○	Images made	○	Internal links
○	Headings	○	Call to action
○	Checked & edited	○	Social media scheduled
○		○	
○		○	

Blog title:

Publish date: **Category:**

Quick Post Summary

What exactly are you aiming for?

Main Keywords

SEO | Pinterest
○ | ○
○ | ○
○ | ○
○ | ○
○ | ○

Opt-in Offer

Are you offering a freebie/upgrade?

Heading #1

Heading #2

Heading #3

Heading #4

Heading #5

Research Points

What research is needed for this?

- ○
- ○
- ○
- ○

Affiliate Products

Are you promoting any products?

- ○
- ○
- ○
- ○

Social Media Plan

What's the social media plan for this?

Blog Post Checklist	
○ Catchy title	○ Descriptions written
○ Keyworded	○ Affiliate links added
○ Images made	○ Internal links
○ Headings	○ Call to action
○ Checked & edited	○ Social media scheduled
○	○
○	○

Blog title:

Publish date: **Category:**

Quick Post Summary — What exactly are you aiming for?

Main Keywords

SEO	Pinterest
○	○
○	○
○	○
○	○
○	○

Opt-in Offer — Are you offering a freebie/upgrade?

Heading #1

Heading #2

Heading #3

Heading #4

Heading #5

Research Points

What research is needed for this?

- ○
- ○
- ○
- ○

Affiliate Products

Are you promoting any products?

- ○
- ○
- ○
- ○

Social Media Plan

What's the social media plan for this?

Blog Post Checklist

○ Catchy title	○ Descriptions written
○ Keyworded	○ Affiliate links added
○ Images made	○ Internal links
○ Headings	○ Call to action
○ Checked & edited	○ Social media scheduled
○	○
○	○

Blog title:

Publish date: **Category:**

Quick Post Summary

What exactly are you aiming for?

Main Keywords

SEO	Pinterest
○	○
○	○
○	○
○	○
○	○

Opt-in Offer

Are you offering a freebie/upgrade?

Heading #1

Heading #2

Heading #3

Heading #4

Heading #5

Research Points

What research is needed for this?

- ○
- ○
- ○
- ○

Affiliate Products

Are you promoting any products?

- ○
- ○
- ○
- ○

Social Media Plan

What's the social media plan for this?

Blog Post Checklist

○ Catchy title	○ Descriptions written
○ Keyworded	○ Affiliate links added
○ Images made	○ Internal links
○ Headings	○ Call to action
○ Checked & edited	○ Social media scheduled
○	○
○	○

Blog title:

Publish date: | **Category:**

Quick Post Summary

What exactly are you aiming for?

Main Keywords

SEO	Pinterest
○	○
○	○
○	○
○	○
○	○

Opt-in Offer

Are you offering a freebie/upgrade?

Heading #1

Heading #2

Heading #3

Heading #4

Heading #5

Research Points

What research is needed for this?

- ○
- ○
- ○
- ○

Affiliate Products

Are you promoting any products?

- ○
- ○
- ○
- ○

Social Media Plan

What's the social media plan for this?

Blog Post Checklist

○ Catchy title	○ Descriptions written
○ Keyworded	○ Affiliate links added
○ Images made	○ Internal links
○ Headings	○ Call to action
○ Checked & edited	○ Social media scheduled
○	○
○	○

Blog title:

Publish date: **Category:**

Quick Post Summary

What exactly are you aiming for?

Main Keywords

SEO	Pinterest
○	○
○	○
○	○
○	○
○	○

Opt-in Offer

Are you offering a freebie/upgrade?

Heading #1

Heading #2

Heading #3

Heading #4

Heading #5

Research Points

What research is needed for this?

- ○
- ○
- ○
- ○

Affiliate Products

Are you promoting any products?

- ○
- ○
- ○
- ○

Social Media Plan

What's the social media plan for this?

Blog Post Checklist	
○ Catchy title	○ Descriptions written
○ Keyworded	○ Affiliate links added
○ Images made	○ Internal links
○ Headings	○ Call to action
○ Checked & edited	○ Social media scheduled
○	○
○	○

	Blog title:

Publish date:	Category:

Quick Post Summary	What exactly are you aiming for?

Main Keywords	SEO	Pinterest
	○	○
	○	○
	○	○
	○	○
	○	○

Opt-in Offer	Are you offering a freebie/upgrade?

Heading #1	
Heading #2	
Heading #3	
Heading #4	
Heading #5	

Research Points

What research is needed for this?

- ○
- ○
- ○
- ○

Affiliate Products

Are you promoting any products?

- ○
- ○
- ○
- ○

Social Media Plan

What's the social media plan for this?

Blog Post Checklist

○ Catchy title	○ Descriptions written
○ Keyworded	○ Affiliate links added
○ Images made	○ Internal links
○ Headings	○ Call to action
○ Checked & edited	○ Social media scheduled
○	○
○	○

◯ Blog title:	

Publish date:	Category:

Quick Post Summary	What exactly are you aiming for?

Main Keywords	SEO ◯ ◯ ◯ ◯ ◯	Pinterest ◯ ◯ ◯ ◯ ◯

Opt-in Offer	Are you offering a freebie/upgrade?

Heading #1	
Heading #2	
Heading #3	
Heading #4	
Heading #5	

Research Points

What research is needed for this?

- ○
- ○
- ○
- ○

Affiliate Products

Are you promoting any products?

- ○
- ○
- ○
- ○

Social Media Plan

What's the social media plan for this?

Blog Post Checklist

○	Catchy title	○	Descriptions written
○	Keyworded	○	Affiliate links added
○	Images made	○	Internal links
○	Headings	○	Call to action
○	Checked & edited	○	Social media scheduled
○		○	
○		○	

	Blog title:	

Publish date:	Category:

Quick Post Summary	What exactly are you aiming for?

Main Keywords	SEO	Pinterest
	○	○
	○	○
	○	○
	○	○
	○	○

Opt-in Offer	Are you offering a freebie/upgrade?

Heading #1	
Heading #2	
Heading #3	
Heading #4	
Heading #5	

Research Points

What research is needed for this?

- ○
- ○
- ○
- ○

Affiliate Products

Are you promoting any products?

- ○
- ○
- ○
- ○

Social Media Plan

What's the social media plan for this?

Blog Post Checklist	
○ Catchy title	○ Descriptions written
○ Keyworded	○ Affiliate links added
○ Images made	○ Internal links
○ Headings	○ Call to action
○ Checked & edited	○ Social media scheduled
○	○
○	○

Blog title:

Publish date: **Category:**

Quick Post Summary

What exactly are you aiming for?

Main Keywords

SEO	Pinterest
○	○
○	○
○	○
○	○
○	○

Opt-in Offer

Are you offering a freebie/upgrade?

Heading #1

Heading #2

Heading #3

Heading #4

Heading #5

Research Points

What research is needed for this?

- ○
- ○
- ○
- ○

Affiliate Products

Are you promoting any products?

- ○
- ○
- ○
- ○

Social Media Plan

What's the social media plan for this?

Blog Post Checklist

○ Catchy title	○ Descriptions written
○ Keyworded	○ Affiliate links added
○ Images made	○ Internal links
○ Headings	○ Call to action
○ Checked & edited	○ Social media scheduled
○	○
○	○

Blog title:

Publish date: **Category:**

Quick Post Summary

What exactly are you aiming for?

Main Keywords

SEO	Pinterest
○	○
○	○
○	○
○	○
○	○

Opt-in Offer

Are you offering a freebie/upgrade?

Heading #1

Heading #2

Heading #3

Heading #4

Heading #5

Research Points

What research is needed for this? ◯

- ○
- ○
- ○
- ○

Affiliate Products

Are you promoting any products?

- ○
- ○
- ○
- ○

Social Media Plan

What's the social media plan for this?

Blog Post Checklist	
○ Catchy title	○ Descriptions written
○ Keyworded	○ Affiliate links added
○ Images made	○ Internal links
○ Headings	○ Call to action
○ Checked & edited	○ Social media scheduled
○	○
○	○

Blog title:

Publish date: **Category:**

Quick Post Summary

What exactly are you aiming for?

Main Keywords

SEO	Pinterest
○	○
○	○
○	○
○	○
○	○

Opt-in Offer

Are you offering a freebie/upgrade?

Heading #1

Heading #2

Heading #3

Heading #4

Heading #5

Research Points

What research is needed for this?

- ○
- ○
- ○
- ○

Affiliate Products

Are you promoting any products?

- ○
- ○
- ○
- ○

Social Media Plan

What's the social media plan for this?

Blog Post Checklist

○ Catchy title	○ Descriptions written
○ Keyworded	○ Affiliate links added
○ Images made	○ Internal links
○ Headings	○ Call to action
○ Checked & edited	○ Social media scheduled
○	○
○	○

Blog title:	

Publish date:	Category:

Quick Post Summary	What exactly are you aiming for?

Main Keywords	SEO	Pinterest
	○	○
	○	○
	○	○
	○	○
	○	○

Opt-in Offer	Are you offering a freebie/upgrade?

Heading #1	
Heading #2	
Heading #3	
Heading #4	
Heading #5	

Research Points

What research is needed for this? ◯

- ○
- ○
- ○
- ○

Affiliate Products

Are you promoting any products?

- ○
- ○
- ○
- ○

Social Media Plan

What's the social media plan for this?

Blog Post Checklist	
○ Catchy title	○ Descriptions written
○ Keyworded	○ Affiliate links added
○ Images made	○ Internal links
○ Headings	○ Call to action
○ Checked & edited	○ Social media scheduled
○	○
○	○

Blog title:	

Publish date:	Category:

Quick Post Summary	What exactly are you aiming for?

Main Keywords	SEO	Pinterest
	○	○
	○	○
	○	○
	○	○
	○	○

Opt-in Offer	Are you offering a freebie/upgrade?

Heading #1	
Heading #2	
Heading #3	
Heading #4	
Heading #5	

Research Points

What research is needed for this?

- ○
- ○
- ○
- ○

Affiliate Products

Are you promoting any products?

- ○
- ○
- ○
- ○

Social Media Plan

What's the social media plan for this?

Blog Post Checklist

○	Catchy title	○	Descriptions written
○	Keyworded	○	Affiliate links added
○	Images made	○	Internal links
○	Headings	○	Call to action
○	Checked & edited	○	Social media scheduled
○		○	
○		○	

Blog title:

Publish date: **Category:**

Quick Post Summary

What exactly are you aiming for?

Main Keywords

SEO	Pinterest
○	○
○	○
○	○
○	○
○	○

Opt-in Offer

Are you offering a freebie/upgrade?

Heading #1

Heading #2

Heading #3

Heading #4

Heading #5

Research Points

What research is needed for this?

- ○
- ○
- ○
- ○

Affiliate Products

Are you promoting any products?

- ○
- ○
- ○
- ○

Social Media Plan

What's the social media plan for this?

Blog Post Checklist	
○ Catchy title	○ Descriptions written
○ Keyworded	○ Affiliate links added
○ Images made	○ Internal links
○ Headings	○ Call to action
○ Checked & edited	○ Social media scheduled
○	○
○	○

Blog title:

Publish date: | **Category:**

Quick Post Summary

What exactly are you aiming for?

Main Keywords

SEO	Pinterest
○	○
○	○
○	○
○	○
○	○

Opt-in Offer

Are you offering a freebie/upgrade?

Heading #1

Heading #2

Heading #3

Heading #4

Heading #5

Research Points

What research is needed for this?

- ○
- ○
- ○
- ○

Affiliate Products

Are you promoting any products?

- ○
- ○
- ○
- ○

Social Media Plan

What's the social media plan for this?

Blog Post Checklist

○ Catchy title	○ Descriptions written
○ Keyworded	○ Affiliate links added
○ Images made	○ Internal links
○ Headings	○ Call to action
○ Checked & edited	○ Social media scheduled
○	○
○	○

Blog title:

Publish date: | **Category:**

Quick Post Summary

What exactly are you aiming for?

Main Keywords

SEO	Pinterest
○	○
○	○
○	○
○	○
○	○

Opt-in Offer

Are you offering a freebie/upgrade?

Heading #1

Heading #2

Heading #3

Heading #4

Heading #5

Research Points

What research is needed for this?

- ◯
- ◯
- ◯
- ◯

Affiliate Products

Are you promoting any products?

- ◯
- ◯
- ◯
- ◯

Social Media Plan

What's the social media plan for this?

Blog Post Checklist

◯ Catchy title	◯ Descriptions written
◯ Keyworded	◯ Affiliate links added
◯ Images made	◯ Internal links
◯ Headings	◯ Call to action
◯ Checked & edited	◯ Social media scheduled
◯	◯
◯	◯

Blog title:

Publish date: **Category:**

Quick Post Summary

What exactly are you aiming for?

Main Keywords

SEO	Pinterest
○	○
○	○
○	○
○	○
○	○

Opt-in Offer

Are you offering a freebie/upgrade?

Heading #1

Heading #2

Heading #3

Heading #4

Heading #5

Research Points

What research is needed for this?

- ○
- ○
- ○
- ○

Affiliate Products

Are you promoting any products?

- ○
- ○
- ○
- ○

Social Media Plan

What's the social media plan for this?

Blog Post Checklist

○ Catchy title	○ Descriptions written
○ Keyworded	○ Affiliate links added
○ Images made	○ Internal links
○ Headings	○ Call to action
○ Checked & edited	○ Social media scheduled
○	○
○	○

Blog title:	

Publish date:	Category:

Quick Post Summary	What exactly are you aiming for?

Main Keywords	SEO	Pinterest
	○	○
	○	○
	○	○
	○	○
	○	○

Opt-in Offer	Are you offering a freebie/upgrade?

Heading #1	
Heading #2	
Heading #3	
Heading #4	
Heading #5	

Research Points

What research is needed for this?

- o
- o
- o
- o

Affiliate Products

Are you promoting any products?

- o
- o
- o
- o

Social Media Plan

What's the social media plan for this?

Blog Post Checklist

o	Catchy title	o	Descriptions written
o	Keyworded	o	Affiliate links added
o	Images made	o	Internal links
o	Headings	o	Call to action
o	Checked & edited	o	Social media scheduled
o		o	
o		o	

Blog title:

Publish date: | **Category:**

Quick Post Summary | What exactly are you aiming for?

Main Keywords

SEO	Pinterest
○	○
○	○
○	○
○	○
○	○

Opt-in Offer | Are you offering a freebie/upgrade?

Heading #1

Heading #2

Heading #3

Heading #4

Heading #5

Research Points

What research is needed for this?

- ○
- ○
- ○
- ○

Affiliate Products

Are you promoting any products?

- ○
- ○
- ○
- ○

Social Media Plan

What's the social media plan for this?

Blog Post Checklist

○ Catchy title	○ Descriptions written
○ Keyworded	○ Affiliate links added
○ Images made	○ Internal links
○ Headings	○ Call to action
○ Checked & edited	○ Social media scheduled
○	○
○	○

	Blog title:

Publish date:	Category:

Quick Post Summary	What exactly are you aiming for?

Main Keywords	SEO	Pinterest
	○	○
	○	○
	○	○
	○	○
	○	○

Opt-in Offer	Are you offering a freebie/upgrade?

Heading #1	
Heading #2	
Heading #3	
Heading #4	
Heading #5	

Research Points

What research is needed for this?

- ◯
- ◯
- ◯
- ◯

Affiliate Products

Are you promoting any products?

- ◯
- ◯
- ◯
- ◯

Social Media Plan

What's the social media plan for this?

Blog Post Checklist	
○ Catchy title	○ Descriptions written
○ Keyworded	○ Affiliate links added
○ Images made	○ Internal links
○ Headings	○ Call to action
○ Checked & edited	○ Social media scheduled
○	○
○	○

Blog title:

Publish date: **Category:**

Quick Post Summary

What exactly are you aiming for?

Main Keywords

SEO	Pinterest
○	○
○	○
○	○
○	○
○	○

Opt-in Offer

Are you offering a freebie/upgrade?

Heading #1

Heading #2

Heading #3

Heading #4

Heading #5

Research Points

What research is needed for this?

- ○
- ○
- ○
- ○

Affiliate Products

Are you promoting any products?

- ○
- ○
- ○
- ○

Social Media Plan

What's the social media plan for this?

Blog Post Checklist

○	Catchy title	○	Descriptions written
○	Keyworded	○	Affiliate links added
○	Images made	○	Internal links
○	Headings	○	Call to action
○	Checked & edited	○	Social media scheduled
○		○	
○		○	

www.ingramcontent.com/pod-product-compliance
Lightning Source LLC
Chambersburg PA
CBHW051209050326
40689CB00008B/1250